# ILLEGALS

by N.A. Homie

First Edition

ISBN (Paperback): 979-8-9998751-0-5

Published by NJI Publishing
Lawrenceville, GA

Printed in the United States of America

For the ones the world tried to erase—
the quiet, the loud,
the exiled, the unheard.
For those who carry identity like armor
and still dare to love out loud.
This is for you.
You are not illegal. You are undeniable.

To my daughter—Saint Michel, and all the
daughters like her...
As you transition into adulthood
may these poems remind you:
you are never too loud, too dark, or too extra.
You are a treasure carved from ancestral cloth.
You don't owe your glory to anyone.

*Illegal is a label made by power.*
*Not a truth born in skin, breath, or birth*

# Table of Contents

# THE SMILE & THE MASK

The first sound is not an explosion—it's a hairline fracture.

Not the kind of break that makes headlines, but the slow, deliberate cracking of a mask worn for years. These poems live in that moment—when the polite smile you've practiced until your jaw ached starts to tremble, when "fitting in" begins to feel like disappearing.

Before I had the language for protest, I had performance—polite nods, the voice I kept on standby for interviews, the way my hair, my name, my tone became bargaining chips for safety.
This section is the sound of that bargain ending. It's the ache and the relief of being done with pretending. It's the spark that jumps when survival chooses truth over silence.

# IF YOU CLAIMED MY HUMANITY

If you claimed my humanity,
you'd have to name the atrocity.
Admit this country thrives on duplicity,
and has shaped its philosophy
around the mistreatment of a brown body—
not to lift it, but twist it into tragedy,
restraining its capacity,
and killing it slowly.

If you claimed my humanity,
you'd have to admit—eventually—
that Alligator Alcatraz ain't fit for human custody.
It's a money pit masked as security,
a breeding ground for state-sanctioned brutality.
And you built it knowingly—
no windows, no mercy,
just heat and your hunger to brand us with inferiority.

You ever watched someone disappear into anonymity?
Not just a silent kind of invisibility—
but swallowed by a system built with enmity,
a bureaucratic swamp masked as civility,
designed to drown them in red tape, guilt-free, with full
impunity.
Where even mosquitoes bite with complicity,
and isolation echoes with hostility.

They call it "processing," a mask for captivity,
a slow erasure framed in civility.
How long can you break me with impunity
before I'm buried in anonymity?
I can smell the mold of neglect—its proximity,
even from here, it reeks of captivity.
I can feel the way that place breathes hostility,

like it's swallowing hope with full complicity.

If you claimed my humanity,
you'd stop pretending this is about security.
Ain't nobody safe in a cage of false civility,
where toilets back up with regularity,
the food infected with worms served with formality,
and tents leak defeat when it rains with no subtlety.
People sweating through clothes in forced humility,
not allowed to change for weeks to reinforce invisibility.

Men swallowed by sanctioned obscurity,
not because they're guilty—
but trapped in a loop of forced passivity,
where silence becomes their new identity.
No charges. Just the wrong time, wrong ethnicity.
Still, they're met with state-sanctioned hostility,
as if survival alone is audacity,
as if the itch from bed bugs is dignity.

If you claimed my humanity,
you'd have to see me in my entirety—
not through the lens of utility,
or policies void of morality.
Not as a border. Not as a threat to your security.
But as a soul shaped by generational gravity.
You'd have to confront your inherited cruelty,
and own your history—not just its pageantry.

I've never stepped foot in that swamp facility,
but I carry its echoes with terrifying clarity.
Each headline fades swallowed by invisibility,
buried beneath the weight of normalized cruelty.
You confuse my silence for stability,
but silence ain't peace—it's complicity.
Another name for state-sanctioned brutality,

another mask over stolen humanity.

If you claimed my humanity,
you'd see in me our shared fragility—
a soul still standing through inherited brutality,
who mourns for strangers out of shared reality.
I know the grief of imposed disparity,
of wounds mapped by forced nationality.
Barbed wire thoughts tighten with tenacity,
but I rise each time, in fierce audacity.

What's the point of claiming my humanity,
if your comfort depends on my invisibility?
If you feast on pain with practiced civility,
while preaching freedom, but funding captivity?
What's the point if truth threatens your fragility,
and you'd rather cage us than face accountability?
You trade compassion for control and cold authority—
just to crown yourself in counterfeit superiority.

If you claimed my humanity,
you'd see this land rotting in its own depravity.
Not just migrants crushed in captivity—
but a country drunk on cruelty's audacity.
Hope's been lynched in broad daylight's clarity,
while justice bleeds out in fake neutrality.
And the badge we call savior?—a masked monstrosity,
feeding the fire of state-born brutality.

# THE MONSTER BEHIND THE SMILE

Welcoming from the profile, I see your smile.
Like a soft lullaby that can ease the tide.
A misleading vibe that says stay for a while—
a warmth that whispers, here your pride won't have to hide.

You turned — and your eyes revealed a hidden file,
A glance laced with judgment, sharp and snide.
That profile grin was crafted to beguile,
To shield the bricks of hate you house inside.

Then I realized behind that smile lives something vile,
A monster cloaked in well-manicured pride.
It greets with warmth but plots my exile,
Its grip tightening each time I turn aside.

Too gay, too Black, too bold to dim my style,
Too wild, too don't-belong-here not to hide.
To you, I'm just another name to put on trial,
But I was born to rise — I soar, I glide.

What happened to you? What broke your profile?
What fed your need for hate to compile?
What trauma taught you to cut and divide?
I ask — like a therapist — hoping to guide.

That's my trauma-informed inquiry before I put you on
trial.
But how fair can it be when the disease runs countrywide?
So deep it leaves no room to reconcile —
It's stitched on the face of a nation that won't let hate
subside.

You clap when I fall—sharp and cold as a crocodile.
You laugh as I bleed, wishing my pain would preside.

6

Still, I ask, though your glare remains hostile:
Will you ever let me stand by your side?

Even though cruelty has long been your lifestyle,
And hatred's the home where you proudly reside,
Do I still coat the wound with a healing vial,
Or call you what you are—a monster with a cruel snide?

## DON'T TOUCH MY HAIR, DON'T TOUCH MY PAIN

I wore my hair in coils today—
tight like fists I unclench for peace,
soft like the history they tried to press out of me.
Still, a hand reached for it—
uninvited, unthinking,
as if I were an exhibit.

But this isn't about hair.
It never really was.

It's about entitlement—
the audacity to touch what was never yours,
no asking, no pause,
as if curiosity cancels consent.

You think you're admiring texture.
What you don't see is what it took to love it—
how long it took to silence that voice:
'You'd be prettier if it were straight.'
You don't see my grandmother burn her scalp
to meet a standard that still spat her out.

You don't see the job interviews,
the stiff smiles, the shifting eyes—
the coded language:
"polished," "professional," "not too ethnic."
You don't see the little Black girl
in the school bathroom, mirror fogged,
tugging at curls someone called "a mess."
That little girl was me.
That little girl is still out there.

So no—

you may not touch my hair,
the crown I shape each morning with care.
You may not touch my pride,
woven through years of silence and stares.
You may not touch my pain,
tender as bruises I've learned to wear.
You may not ask me what I'm mixed with,
because my hair's fineness doesn't fit
the picture you've painted of what *coilness* should be.

Because every strand you reach for
is rooted in something sacred—
not just texture, but testimony—
something I've earned
through fire, through shame,
something we're still reclaiming.

Touching it like a novelty
makes a mockery of the journey.
You want to feel it?
Feel the weight of being told your natural isn't enough.
Feel the silence that follows
when we speak truth too loud for comfort.

I am not your curiosity.
Not your access point to Blackness.
Not your touchable moment.

So when I say,
Don't touch my hair,
what I mean is:
Don't touch my history.
Don't touch my dignity.
Don't touch my right to exist—freely.

And when I say,

Don't touch my pain—
I mean: don't minimize it.
Don't exoticize it.
Don't say you love us
without loving the fight it took
to love ourselves.

## THE INTERVIEW VOICE

I used to rehearse it—not in a glass,
but in the echo of my mother's tone.
"Enunciate. Smile. Let the stammer pass.
Don't fidget. And never go alone.
You don't get second chances, choose your cues—
not when you're walking in borrowed shoes."

The voice I use in interviews
isn't mine—it's just a loan.
A softened echo polished not to offend.
Airbrushed in a neutral tone.
to sound like I belong, composed and grown—
but never too much, never my own.

Gone are the roots of my accent's sway,
the rhythm of my grandmother's lullabies.
The spice of 'too much culture'—scrubbed away,
each vibrant note reduced to compromise.
I lace my words like old dress shoes—tight,
polished for show, but never quite right.

I don't just code-switch—I disappear,
swallowing parts they'll never see.
To sound less foreign, less unclear,
less like the stories on their TV.
They call me polished. They call me bright.
But never ask what I lost to sound "right."

Like I should be grateful just to stay still,
as if survival were a marketable skill.
I water down my résumé to dim the flame,
clip leadership so I don't outshine.
Dull the brilliance to keep me tame—
because excellence can be seen as crime.

I round the edges that scream too loud.
Though I've worked twice as hard, the rewards still fade.
I shrink myself—not overqualified and proud—
but because I've seen doors slam, sharp and slick,
On those who never learned the trick.

I'm not here to steal your job or pride,
Just trying to feed my kin, keep hope alive.
I tiptoe so your comfort won't collide,
They never ask what hunger I survive—
If I skipped meals to make this start,
Or borrowed this blazer like borrowed heart.

They don't ask if I'm the eldest hope, the guide,
The one who translates, holds it all tight.
These shoes I wear—too small, too wide—
Pinch every step I take toward "right."
Each blister whispers what I've concealed:
That even acceptance comes pain-sealed.

I wear the mask. I toe the line.
I speak like struggle's not my kin.
Each word rehearsed to sound just fine,
Each posture trained to tuck me in.
I bend like I've never cracked or wept—
But even silence leaves secrets unkept.


And still—I leave, unsure they saw me whole,
or just a shine, a shadow in their room.
Polished shoes don't speak the soul,
they just reflect what's been assumed.
They want excellence trimmed to please—
soft-spoken, well-mannered, and eager to appease.

# RESUMÉ'S EDGES

I trim my triumphs like split ends,
shave down my titles, smooth what offends—
sand off the grit where my fights begin.

The late-night shifts, the double grind,
language barriers I learned to unwind,
unpaid translation duties framed as kindness.

Translator, cook, and eldest scout—
the one who knew what forms were about,
who read between the lines and went without.

I remove the "why" behind my resilience,
afraid they'll mistake it for over-brilliance—
like I'm trying too hard to earn this existence.

I delete lifelong skills—"immigrant hustle,"
"eldest daughter resilience," the daily juggle—
"led siblings through storms without a scuffle."

These skills don't fit in bullet points—
a childhood shaped by fractured joints,
by hands that learned to mend disjoints.

I've been told: keep it clean.
Make it corporate. Make it lean.
Trim your soul to fit the machine.

But how do you reduce a life of scraping joy from scarcity,
into one page, double-spaced, with quiet disparity?
Where struggle's trimmed to meet corporate clarity.

My résumé has edges, that's the proof,
because I've lived where paper cuts

don't bleed ink, but sacrifice—and truth.

So if I come off sharp, it's because I've learned—
not for praise, not to be affirmed,
but because I've bled where paper burned.

And no, I won't dull myself to be digestible.
I won't shrink just to keep things comfortable.
My truth resists your need for approval—unyielding,
indivisible.

## CODE-SWITCHING ISN'T SURVIVAL —
## IT'S EXHAUSTION

I wear my mask like Sunday church clothes—pressed and
plain,
tailored to quiet my thunder, conceal my rain.
Each vowel clipped, every tone rehearsed—
my real voice buried, my truth reversed.

Tuck the Creole, flatten the español,
polish my "hi's" and soften my soul.
Hide the rhythm in my accent's rise,
mask the sun that lives behind my eyes.

I can't "just be myself" anywhere,
when myself gets side-eyed for being too loud,
too proud, too nappy, too round—
too much for rooms never built for me to stay.

When I enter your room, I tuck parts of me away,
like contraband joy I'm not allowed to display.
My walk is trimmed, my shoes laced tight,
my mask pulled snug—yet it fits just right—
for blending in, for being seen,
but never too heard, never too keen.

They praise the poise but miss the cost—
each twisted syllable, something lost.
Each practiced smile is time I spend
breaking my back so you don't bend.

This isn't grace—it's exhaustion's art,
the daily erasure of a beating heart.
And still, I show up: Black and bold,
in rooms that chill what I long to hold.

Because code-switching isn't strategy—
it's the mask I mastered out of need.
It's oppression wrapped in quiet tragedy.
Damn—code-switching isn't survival, it's exhaustion.

# TRENDING TRUTHS

The only constant in America is change.
Not the kind rooted in freedom or truth,
but the kind that decides where justice belongs.
Not grounded in facts, but bartered in power and trade.
On a Tuesday morning, it seems people care,
but by midday, we're footnotes—quickly forgotten.

Who we are—the cause—can shift with the wind, quickly
forgotten.
It can vanish as fast as profits or polls shift, or as trends
change.
A performance of justice disguised as performative care—
It was only yesterday they spoke of D.E.I. like it was
gospel truth.
But the real work? That stayed hidden—buried in unspoken
trade.
They said "inclusive" like it was the space where everyone
belongs.

It was all a farce—justice auctioned in the name of trade.
For five seconds, they wanted to be gay, trans—like they
care.
Performative posts dressed up as a search for truth,
like saying "they/them" could resurrect the forgotten.
While secretly asking if our existence really belongs,
it was trending to clap for identity, then beg for change.

We're back to being punchlines. They no longer care.
And ICE waits to shove you back where injustice belongs.
Speak with a shadowed tongue, they'll question your truth.
We're no longer the quota or the treat—just the forgotten.
All that talk about accents being "exotic"? That's the
change.
Now intolerance is the more rewarding trade.

The only space they save for you? Border patrol's brutal trade.
You're still bleeding, but the crowd already stopped pretending to care.
The only constant in this country is trending change.
If your English is imperfect, there's no place your brilliance belongs.
Five seconds of spotlight—then you're back to being forgotten.
So tell me—who gives two fucks about being on the side of truth?

What's trending today fades fast—such is the sad truth.
But the damage lingers in courts where there's no fair trade.
You're left bleeding when your sponsorship dries up— forgotten.
It stings when they cut the funding that once looked like care.
It echoes when the world moves on, as if your story never belongs.
Because the only constant in this country is change.

You barter truth for trend, but your trade is hollow.
What you called care left the rest of us forgotten.
Still, we rise—rooted in change, in power, in where our voice belongs.

# BLACK SQUARE DIDN'T SAVE US

We watched you go quiet
for exactly one day.
Posted a square so black
it matched the silence that followed.
No caption. No context.
Just your digital virtue—cropped and filtered.

You called it solidarity.
We called it a square
because that's how it felt—
boxed in,
bordered,
easy to delete.

You said it was to amplify Black voices.
But all we heard was echo—
your voice,
your click,
your silence.

You didn't call your senator.
Didn't call your cousin out at dinner.
Didn't call back when we needed backup.
You just called it "allyship"
and moved on.

You thought we'd be grateful
for your pixelated performance—
like a square could shoulder
the centuries of chains,
the knees on necks,
the schools redlined, and dreams declined.

You followed the blackout trend

but never showed up
when the lights came back on.

Your square was not a shield.
It didn't stop the bullets,
the bans,
the biases baked into policies
you've never had to question.

It was a box you checked.
A bandage on your conscience.
A placeholder for the work
you never planned to do.

Because when the algorithm shifted,
so did you.
When the mood changed,
so did your message.
When we cried again,
you were back to brunch.

Black squares didn't save us.
They saved you—
from feeling complicit.
From doing more.
From doing anything.

And maybe that was the point all along.

# GREEN CARDS DON'T MEAN GO

Yo—
I'm fresh with that new swag: my green card.
Thinking I'm done with USCIS—
fully legal now,
queen of my block,
pocket paper screaming I belong.

Until 6 o'clock news hits—
there's José
pinned to pavement,
ICE cuffing him
for speaking too much Spanglish
at the wrong time
in the wrong zip code.

Twenty years legal.
Still got slammed.
Still got questioned.
Still got ghosted by justice.

That's when it hit—

A green card don't mean go.
It means—
"Be on your best behavior."
"Spell your name the same every time."
"Don't blink too fast at customs."


It's not a prize.
It's a permission slip you can lose
for being too loud, too queer,
too poor, too foreign,
or simply

too tired.

They said "welcome,"
but meant—
"Be grateful."
"Don't ask for too much."
"Don't talk about race or politics—
unless it makes us look just."

Green card ≠ green light.
It's more like:
"Flashing yellow.
Borderline red.
Borderline gone.
Always under review."

And don't you dare forget—
they know your mama's address.
The one back home, wrapped in stress,
you were told to leave behind
like a bad habit,
like a foreign mess.

But how can you forget a place
that still sends prayers
in the folded creases of money orders?
That still believes you've made it—
that success means borders,
not the bruises you keep hidden under folders.
that thinks your plastic sheen
means you're finally clean.

Green card?
It means you can work.
But not breathe easy.
Not complain.

Not protest.
Not "make waves."
Not fully belong.
Not sing your song.
Not prove them wrong.

It means:
"Stay in line. Stay small. Stay silent."

But baby—
I got papers,
and I still got questions:
like why freedom
feels like sanction,
a probation sentence
with no court date… no direction.

# I'M NOT YOUR QUIET BLACK GIRL

I'm not your quiet Black girl in a floral dress
Not your grateful-to-be-here, excusing your stress
Not your smile-and-nod, trained to suppress

Not your spiritual mammy in a midi dress
Whispering affirmations while you drain me, nonetheless
My rage is too loud, my flame too fierce to suppress

I don't shrink in boardrooms under duress
I don't flatten my voice to ease your distress
I don't tame my hair or my rage to impress

I was raised to vanish through the night's darkness
In case thieves, kidnappers, or your kin broke in, no less
A little girl taught to sleep light, trained by unrest

I survived worse than bedtime story darkness
Yet I rise with the sun, despite anxiety's excess
Ready to face the shit life hurls—relentless

I'm not your typical Black girl in Sunday dress
Trauma's my twin, and I carry it with finesse
I fight for tomorrow, even under duress

My past is part of my unlucky birthright—no need for
redress.
It carved a spine laced with quiet boldness.
Now I burn bright enough to torch their guess.

So no, I'm not your quiet Black girl in Sunday dress,
Not the one performing just to earn your impress.
I won't twist or plead for access.

I don't dance to your tune—I command the fitness.

I make the beats that shake your stillness.
I move the room with unbothered prowess.

You don't get to name me, contain me, or mold me to
impress.
Your box was never built to hold this boldness.
I blaze beyond your frame—untamed, no less.

# BORDERS BENEATH OUR SKIN

A border is not only a line on a map—it can live inside a body.

It's in the pause before someone says your name. In the hesitation before you say it yourself. In the way your own tongue reshapes itself for safety. These poems carry the maps etched into our skin: accents that carry oceans, scars that tell whole migrations, memories folded small enough to fit in a pocket. They are stories of visas that expire, papers that measure worth, and homes that must be defended every day.

But they are also love letters—to those still waiting, still fighting, still here. Because the truth is this: you are more than your paperwork, more than your silence, and you belong without permission.

## ENGLISH WAS MY FOURTH LANGUAGE, PAIN WAS MY FIRST

I learned English
watching Springer, Maury, Cheaters, then Oprah—
chaos and gospel, side by side,
chairs flying like curses, truths colliding,
while I sat wide-eyed, notebook open like a prayer.

More importantly,
I read books with a dictionary in my lap,
highlighting words like winning numbers—
each one a shot at fluency.
I once spent a week thinking affection
meant infection,
'cause I mixed up the pages.

I'd sound out syllables
like tasting soup I wasn't sure was done—
slow, cautious,
tongue curling, tripping
over S's, over TH's—
each sound a pothole I hadn't learned to dodge.

At school, I learned articulate
was code for unexpected.
A compliment—meant to correct me
not praise me.
Teachers grinned too wide
when I conjugated better
than kids they called the brightest—
as if fluency had snuck in
wearing a brown face.

I'm still waiting for your favorite line:
"Where did you learn to speak so well?"

"Where were you educated to sound so beautiful?"
As if my vocabulary were a party trick—
not a lifeline.
Not survival.

I didn't just learn English—
I inhaled it.
Swallowed whole dictionaries
hoping they'd make me easier to love,
harder to deport,
less likely to be labeled a threat
in a room full of whiteness.

And still,
pain stayed fluent—
always first to speak,
never needing a repeat,
never lost in translation.

Pain said
keep quiet at the doctor's office
unless you want your mama embarrassed.
Pain said
don't speak too fast,
they'll think you're hiding something.

Pain said
"trilingual" don't pay more,
just makes them ask
"Can you say that again, but in English?"
even when you already did.

I learned English
with a side of shame,
grit,
and immigrant guilt.

The language wrapped itself around my tongue
like a flag and a noose,
depending on who was listening.

Now I speak three languages
and think in four,
and still,
I hesitate before asking for help,
'cause I remember
what it feels like to be laughed at
for mispronouncing "comfortable."

I write books now—
not just to be heard
but to remind myself
that my voice
has always been
worth listening to.

And even now, I still remember—
English came fourth,
pain was my first.

# MY ACCENT IS NOT AN APOLOGY

My accent is not an apology—
not baggage, shame, or pathology.
It's mango-sweet, pepper-strong,
a rhythm where my roots belong.

It's market chatter, Sunday choirs,
the hiss of oil, ancestral fires.
It's lullabies in borrowed rooms,
it's joy and grief in echoed wombs.

Each syllable stitched in layered skies
too rich for walls, too vast for lies.
This voice holds spice, and sea, and soul—
it speaks to make the broken whole.

Not here to polish off my name,
nor let your labels stake their claim.
Every vowel you call "incorrect"
still carries truths you won't detect.

You guess my home by what I say,
as if all Blackness wears one way.
But I am not your pet to train,
nor here to scrub what you disdain.

You say, "Speak clearly"; I hear, "Erase."
I won't whitewash my native base.
I speak for those still pushing through—
my voice was never built for you.

And if my tone makes you uneasy,
know I am not here to make it easy.
My accent stands, fierce and free—

a world beyond what you can see.

# SUGAR AND SLAP

My first backhanded compliment—dipped in praise, but
soaked in racism—
came from a college professor.
"You write so well… for a foreigner."
She smiled when she said it, like her praise was a gift,
as if my words were rare, my syntax some myth.

Like brilliance required a passport stamp.
Like metaphors from my mouth should limp.
As if I had trespassed into eloquence.

She asked to use my craft—her voice warm, rehearsed—
to show the class what excellence looked like.
And for a moment, I felt seen. Almost whole.
Until the spotlight burned too bright, and I realized—
that was my first taste of microaggression,
my welcome to Racism 1101.

Then began my journey of swallowing sugar and slaps,
smiling at applause wrapped tight in velvet traps.
This country loves to praise but never lift—
handing thorned bouquets just to watch them drift.

What does "foreigner" have to do with prose?
What does my ascent steal from what I know?
Why must my syntax be a miracle that defies gravity?
Is this the academic version of
"You're so pretty… for a dark-skinned girl"?
The classroom echo of "Wow, you speak so well"?
Why is my eloquence your biggest surprise?
Why is your praise always dressed in disguise?

Each step I take, you tarnish with doubt.
You say I'm bright—but leave the brilliance out.

My skin, my accent, my birth—you treat as a test,
as if rising at all means I stole from your nest.

"You're doing so well... as an immigrant."
"You're so smart... for someone like you."
You've seen my ancestors' glory, yet you still chant
the same old praise—just wrapped in something new.

My first backhanded compliment came from a college
professor—
as if Black, immigrant, and articulate can't cohabitate.
What you call praise, I've learned to decode—
a sugar-laced weapon, a backhanded ode.

You dissect me kindly—smile, applaud, erase—
expecting my genius to arrive in a palatable face.
But I'm not here for your softened racism,
not here to be the safe taste of activism.

And still, you wonder why I don't bow.
Still, you ask, Why not now?
But I've known the sting behind the sweet,
and I don't need applause to know I'm complete.

## YOU STILL MATTER

They told you
paper made you human—
legality is your dignity,
and borderlines on a map
determined your worth.

But you—
you mattered before their borders.
Before El Salvador's prisons took you in.
Before Louisiana jails erased your name.
Before ICE stamped Otay Mesa
as your final destination.

You matter still.

Even when they left you
drinking toilet water
at Alligator Alcatraz.
When the worms arrived
before the breakfast tray.
When they labeled your painful screams
"noncompliance,"
and your panic—a "threat."

You still matter.

Even when they dumped you in detention
on a continent you've never seen—
sent to Ghana
for speaking broken English
with a Caribbean tilt.
Even when ICE forgot
you were a father,
a daughter,

a human being.

You matter still.

Even when you collapsed
in the Sonoran desert,
running toward survival.
When they found you—
after the buzzards.

Even when your family grieves
in silence—
no grave,
no answers,
no justice—

You mattered.

You matter.
Not because of paperwork,
or fluent English,
or waiting your turn in a broken line.
You matter because you breathed.
Because you dreamed.
Because your heart kept beating
in a world that refused
to call you by name.

You were not born illegal.
No one is.
You were made to feel that way.

And to us,
you are not disposable.
You are not forgotten.
You are not alone.

You mattered.
You still do.

# GHOST IN THE SWAMP

From Africa to the Americas, dragged in chains from coast
to coast—
We became panteras, hunted, unnamed from coast to coast.

Lost in the swamp like ancestral ghosts.

From Haiti, Mexico, and El Salvador's shore,
to Florida's echo, still they demand more.

Lost in the swamp like ancestral ghosts.

Our sweat built roofs, they now live beneath,
Our tongues are proofs, of laws they twist in their teeth.

Lost in the swamp like ancestral ghosts.

We picked their fruit, filled every hand
Yet still they root, go back to your land.

Lost in the swamp like ancestral ghosts.

The swamp knows—names they still try to erase,
Buried in flames —and memory's grace.

Lost in the swamp like ancestral ghosts.

Mangroves whisper— what borders regret,
We bled through the blister—we're not done yet.

Lost in the swamp like ancestral ghosts.

My uncle's hands bled—but were calloused with hope,
his slicing machete led— through sugarcane rope.

Lost in the swamp like ancestral ghosts.

Mama's silence trembled—she signed with fear,
Each line assembled—praying ICE won't appear.

Lost in the swamp like ancestral ghosts.

Chain-link fences, and cages don't just divide,
They choke all sentences, where dreams once tried.

Lost in the swamp like ancestral ghosts.

We are the haunted, the unclaimed kin,
Seeking *passports-vaulted*, to the skin we're in.

Lost in the swamp like ancestral ghosts.

No matter how much we give—how much we make,
They sift how we live—then twist what they take.

Lost in the swamp like ancestral ghosts.

Our worth weighed down— by their mythic tale
Their fabled crown— their rigged holy grail.

Lost in the swamp like ancestral ghosts.

So we search for, the ghost of origins past,
For soil that holds us ashore, for roots that last.

Lost in the swamp like ancestral ghosts.

But home isn't always the land, where the foot first fell
It's the place we land, we fight to exist and dwell.

Lost in the swamp like ancestral ghosts.

From Africa to the Americas, dragged in chains from coast
to coast—
We became Panteras, hunted, unnamed from coast to coast.

Lost in the swamp like ancestral ghosts.

## FILE UNDER: OTHER

You heard my name and closed the case
no brilliance, grit, or "she can't keep pace."
Filed me as "Other," less-than-bright,
before I had a chance to write.

Your ears switched off mid-sentence, heard
the hint of "foreign," judgment stirred.
You smiled like policy, labeled me slow
a patient, not a doc in coat.

You asked me where I'm "really" from,
while you botched my name in every syllable.
You held your doubt like settled law
as if my voice proved my invisible flaws

You read my pause as empty space,
not choosing words to guard your face.
You called my quiet proof I lacked
I weighed the truth and chose intact.

Thanks for the clarity you gave
how low you rank those you won't save.
You showed me fast, in record time,
your prejudice dressed up as rhyme.

No CV line, no published page
could move you past your little cage.
To you I'm always just a guess
a riddle zipped in borrowed dress.

Your desk is a gate, your grin a wall;
your meetings, one long mirrored hall.
I brought a hammer of proof and truth
but barely made a window in your roof.

And yes, I used to make myself small,
rehearse-the-smile, agree-with-all
until I learned the door stays shut
unless you shoulder through the cut.

But guess again: I pulled your file,
struck the match and walked the mile.
The road was long—look where I'm near:
not smaller—sharper, crystal-clear.

I kept my name. I passed your test.
I wear this voice like Sunday's best
not on approval, not on loan
a cadence carved and wholly owned.

I built the dreams you overlooked,
in dialects you never booked.
Each time I speak, I loosen a key
unlock a thousand tongues like me.

# WHO DO I CALL

Who do I call
when the protector becomes the abuser,
when the one with the loudest "freedom" chant
tightens the noose—
behind closed doors?

Who do I dial
when I can't call 911—
because they're the ones
dragging children by the wrists,
slamming mothers against steel,
deporting fathers like forgotten luggage?

Who do I look up to
for a glimmer of hope
when even the sky turns its face—
while heat scorches through tin roofs
of holding cells that smother humanity?

When detention means
being stripped of both name and nation.
Spanish tongue, dropped in Senegal.
Korean blood, dumped in Kinshasa.
Your File stamped: Other.
Your Humanity: still under review.

Who sounds the alarm
when hope dies in holding tanks,
when despair tastes like powdered eggs
and reused underwear?

Who screams this is not okay
when the silent ones
once screamed for Syria,

wept for Ukraine,
marched for Myanmar,
but go mute
when the cruelty creeps
from sea to shining sea?

There is a kind of malice
in bureaucratic violence—
a pleasure in paper cuts
that slice families apart.
They hide behind their hoods
clutching headsets, hiding behind badges
issuing silence like a threat.

I ask again—
Who do I call
when the law grins wide
as it ships you off
to a country
you've only traced on maps?

Who do I call
when death starts whispering
like mercy—
softer than this waiting
with no end in sight?

## YOUR LAWS WERE NEVER FOR ME

I am not lawless.
I was born into laws
that never meant to include me.
Laws written in ink that faded
when it touched brown skin.

I was taught to "follow the rules,"
but the rules kept shifting—
lines redrawn while we were sleeping,
dreams slipping through cracks we kept sweeping,
doors locked after we translated the signs.

They told me:
"Just get your papers."
As if that ever meant protection.
As if their system was a fair game,
some passported affection
and not a roulette with our lives.

But I am not of this land.
I am of the ones plowed under it.
Because my land was bled to bloom yours
500,000 in gold, stolen under gunpoint
from Haitian vaults,
shipped to the U.S.A. while we were told
it was for our "protection."
They stole our soil, then wrote the clause—
weed fields burned, elections bought,
insurgents paid in foreign tongues.
And still, they say we are the danger.

I come from a place
where prayers travel in remittance receipts
where mothers teach resilience

with empty pots and steady hands.
Their silence fed demands
they never dared repeat.
And still—
you ask me to shrink
inside your laws?
You criminalize survival
and call it justice.
You erase histories
and call it merit.

But I remember.
I remember the checkpoints,
the cages,
their laws inked on quiet pages,
the silence when we begged for mercy.

I remember your laws
were never made to uplift me—
only to fold me,
only to hold me back.

So I walk with ghosts beside me—
papers in hand,
no land where I stand,
questions in heart,
and I wonder daily:

What is the cost of belonging
in a country that only knows
how to take—
how to fake
its welcome with flags and laws it will break?

So we carry what they tried to erase—
not just papers, but names,

but prayers,
but stories carved in hunger and grace.
Even if they never gave us a place,
we became the map.

We make our own constitution
out of survival.
Draft resolution,
pass amendments
with every breath
we refuse to hold.

# THE LETTER HOME I'LL NEVER SEND

Dear Maman,
Today I almost wrote you—
but I didn't know how to explain
that I'm still working
the three jobs I said I left months ago
because neither pays enough
for me to have just one.

I didn't want to tell you
I've been eating instant noodles again,
not because I love them,
but because they're cheap
and don't remind me of home.

You keep asking for pictures—
of the house you think I bought,
the car you assumed was mine,
the "new life" I said I was building.
But truth is,
I've mastered the art
of taking photos with clean corners
and hiding the cracked parts.

You still believe
America is paved with gold,
but I'm walking on gravel,
dodging ICE and rent hikes,
worrying more about
my name on a lease
than my name on a degree.

I never told you
about the time I was followed
on my way home from work,

or how the police asked for my papers
like I was a package
they could return to sender.

Maman,
I speak English now,
but it doesn't mean they listen.
I pay taxes
but still feel undocumented
in every room where I say
"yes, sir"
and "I understand,"
even when I don't.

I wish I could ask
how you managed so much with so little—
how you fed us faith
when there was barely flour.
I carry your strength,
but some days
it feels like it's cracking in my hands.

The truth is,
I don't write
because I no longer know
in what language to convey
a dream deferred so long
it forgot how to pronounce hope.

So instead,
I send silence
wrapped in Western Union,
hoping the money
says what I can't:
I'm still trying.

Love,
Your child who made it out
but has yet to find a home.

# THE SPARKS WE CARRY

We have all seen it—the way the world burns for us one week, then forgets us the next.

There's a particular grief in being turned into a hashtag. To watch your pain go viral, then vanish. To hear your name spoken like a slogan instead of a prayer.

These poems are the embers that survive after the noise. They remember who stayed loud when the cameras left, who kept building when the march was over, who carried the flame when the crowd moved on. They are proof that justice is not seasonal, care is not a trend, and our stories still burn even when the headlines go dark.

# QUEER IN CHURCH CLOTHES

Have you ever met a Haitian lesbian?
Neither had I—
not in daylight.
We exist,
but most of us live in a closet with no door,
no lock, no key—
just shadows thick enough to disappear in.
We're free only at night,
or when no one's watching.
The moment the world flips on the light,
we slip back into silence like it's armor.

Ever met a gay Haitian man?
Maybe.
He's the one who laughs while bleeding.
The one who gets roasted at dinner
and still clears the plates.
He's been told,
"Ou pa vrèman masisi—it's a spirit, a curse."
"Nou pral lage ou nan legliz, Bondye ap mete w sou wout."
That's because we come from a culture
where queerness is either mocked
or diagnosed—
a sickness they swear the church can cure,
or worse,
a voudou spell—
 to be prayed off.

I've met queer Haitians.
We learned how to survive
beneath church hats and starched collars,
fluent in coded silence.
We loved in shadows
and performed holiness under fluorescent light.

The only silver lining I packed
when I left home
was the hope that here,
finally,
I could peel off the church clothes.
But that illusion hit like a slap—
when I saw some of y'all smile in my face
just to cut me clean from behind.
Because I'm no longer marketable.
Because queer
don't trend like it used to.

I've come to prefer the ones back home—
the ones who laughed while they judged.
At least their ignorance walked through the front door.
Not like here,
where applause is plastic,
and silence slices deeper than shame.

But I'm still here.
Still queer.
Still sacred—
even in stitched and starched salvation.

# WHAT THE F*CK IS THE GAY AGENDA?

You say gay rights are a threat.
But I ask—a threat to what?
To your comfort, wrapped in ignorance?
To the silence you mistake for peace?
To the illusion that sameness equals safety?

You say kids shouldn't see "gay shit."
I ask—what is "gay shit"?
Is it love, unboxed and unashamed?
Is it someone existing
without apology, without erasure, without your permission?

You say being gay is taught.
But I ask—where are these lessons?
What blackboard holds the curriculum
that says, "Be gay for extra credit"?
Show me the teacher handing out rainbows like report
cards.

You said, "My imagined kids shouldn't see rainbows."
I ask, "Do actual kids question the flag?
Do stars and stripes whisper conquest?
Do they pledge allegiance to imperialism
just because red, white, and blue hangs in the hallway?"

You said, "But what if trauma makes someone gay?"
I said, "So now you blame rape victims?
You call identity a scar?
You think queerness blooms from bruises—
not from truth, not from being?"

You say there's a gay agenda.
But I ask—what's the straight agenda?
Is it mom and dad on every cereal box?

Is it the kiss on the porch before work?
Is it prom kings and princess-cut rings?

You say exposure makes someone queer.
But I ask—if that's true,
how did so many of us bloom
from your straight homes,
your judgmental churches,
your straight-line streets?

You say you're protecting kids.
But I ask—From what?
From love?
From visibility?
From the mirror
that dares to show them themselves?

You say, "What if they see it and turn?"
I say, "What if they see it—and feel seen?"
What if the agenda isn't corruption,
but compassion?
Not conversion,
but truth?

So what the fuck is the gay agenda?
Here it is—
To live.
To breathe.
To exist without erasure.
To stop shrinking for your comfort.
To stop begging for rights
we should've had all along.

That's the agenda.
And if that offends you,

maybe it's not the rainbow
that needs rethinking.

# I'M NOT YOUR GAY BEST FRIEND

I'm not your gay best friend.
Not your sassy sidekick,
your brunch-hour accessory,
your after-hours entertainment
to prove how "open-minded" you are—
when the lights go dim
and the cameras start rolling.

I'm not your only Black friend either—
so don't come asking me to translate TikToks,
or sweeten your white guilt
in a group chat full of silence
and carefully curated memes.

What do you mean I "don't sound Black"?
What does Black sound like to you—
trauma, struggle,
incomplete sentences?

Do you hear my vocabulary
and think I must've swallowed whiteness—
just because I code-switch
better than your Wi-Fi?

Language has no color.
But your ignorance bleeds—
red, white,
and gaslight.

I'm not your trophy friend—
not the rainbow on your diversity badge,
not the checkbox you tick on inclusion forms.
Not the proof you flash
to dodge accountability.

I don't owe you my coming out confession.
You never had to explain your own expression.
So why must my truth be dissected, displayed,
like a warning label or a moral transgression?

No, I don't want you.
Being gay doesn't mean I'm into you.
That fantasy? Yours—not mine.
And even if I was…
you wouldn't survive me.

You don't get to parade my pain
for pity claps or shallow gain.
Don't smile in my face, then turn to chat—
where my truth becomes your backstage act.

You say you're an ally.
But allyship doesn't come
with applause,
with trend cycles,
with a costume you dust off for June.

It comes with listening.
With unlearning.
With knowing when to shut up—
and stay shut
when your voice isn't needed.

So no—
I'm not your best gay friend.
Not your magical negro.
Not your intersectional experiment
for clout and conversations you're too scared to lead.

I'm a whole human.
Messy. Loud. Beautiful. Unapologetic.

I don't need your "acceptance"—
just for you to stay out of my way.

## ACCEPTANCE AIN'T A FAVOR

I don't need your acceptance—no pass, no slip, no script.
I don't need your acceptance—no pass, no slip, no script.
This ain't a favor, it's my life. Stop acting like I tripped.

You say you can love me—but not respect how I live.
You say you can love me—but not respect how I live.
That ain't love, baby—that's the lie you always give.

You welcome me with silence, then whisper behind your
grin.
You welcome me with silence, then whisper behind your
grin.
That ain't kindness; it's control stitched in Sunday skin.

You fear our kind of freedom, like joy's a goddamn threat.
You fear our kind of freedom, like joy's a goddamn threat.
We're just kissing in daylight—no shame, no regret.

You act like respect's a prize, like you're the one to choose.
You act like respect's a prize, like you're the one to choose.
But I was whole long before you ever laced up your shoes.

That "but" in your sentence? Yeah, that's your confession.
That "but" in your sentence? Yeah, that's your confession.
It's where your fear hides—still praying for suppression.

I ain't your pet project, your Pride Month display.
I ain't your pet project, your Pride Month display.
I'm not your test run just 'cause the headlines say it's okay.

So fold up your fake kindness, your tolerance worn thin.
So fold up your fake kindness, your tolerance worn thin.
Keep it for yourself; I'm already whole within.

# THIS BODY WILL NOT BE ERASED

This body—
made of flesh, fire, and memory—
will not be erased.

Not by your laws,
your dress codes
your silence drills,
your bathroom bills,
your borderlines drawn in red.

This body walks into rooms
already judged,
already juried—
yet it dares to speak
in a voice that won't break
or beg for translation.

You try to fold me small—
into checkboxes that can't hold my curves,
into pronouns that peel like old stickers,
into roles designed to erase me
in plain sight.

But this body?
It ain't your blank slate.
It's battleground and birthright,
a holy site, a survival map.
It wears scars like signatures—
not wounds,
but witness.

This body has danced
even when grief was the DJ.
It has loved

in defiance of doctrine.
It has survived—
not because you let it,
but because it refused
to leave quietly.


And when you tell me
to cover up, to sit still, to blend in—
I remember my ancestors
who were told the same,
but walked out of shackles
wearing nothing but truth.

So don't call me brave
just for existing.
Call me necessary.
Call me nationless.
Call me yours—
only if you claim every part of me.

Because this body,
in all its bold, Black, queer, immigrant,
sun-kissed contradictions—
will not be scrubbed from
your history books
or your line of sight.

This body will not be erased.
It will be etched
into the memory of every place
that tried—
and failed—
to make me disappear.

# THEY TRIED TO BREAK ME BEAUTIFUL

They tried to break me
beautiful—
cut me down
into a shape they could name.
Soft enough to smile on cue,
hard enough to take the blame.

They said,
"Tone it down."
"Straighten that curl."
"Your hips are a weapon—
don't take up the world."

They called it praise
when they said I was exotic—
called it love
while bleaching the tropic
right out of my skin.
But I've never been
Your delicate thing.

I am flesh,
not for sale.
I am curves—
not a cautionary tale.
My thighs don't apologize
for thunder.
My nose is wide like history—
and I won't go under.

You saw power—called it too loud.
Saw beauty—called it too proud.
Tried to frame me in museum glass,
but I cracked the case

with every laugh.

Because pretty never saved me—
not when they raided our homes,
not when they dragged my cousin
from a checkpoint alone.
Not when I sat silent
through "compliments"
from men who knew
my quiet wasn't consent—
just survival.

They tried to break me
into fragments
they could use—
a muse,
a token,
a caution sign.
But I was never yours to refine.

I grew in the shadows
of aunties who wore grief
like eyeliner—
who taught me beauty
ain't in the mirror,
but in the fire
you still carry
after the world tries to burn you
graceful.

So no—
I won't be still.
Won't be tame.
Won't shrink to fit
a hashtag name.

I'm not here
to be your proof
that pain makes pearls.

I'm here to say:
You don't have to break to be beautiful.
But if you were,
you still are.

## YOU CALLED ME ANGRY—I CALL ME FREE

You called me angry—
because I spoke with a spine,
because my voice held steady
when I said, "No. Not *today*, *That's mine*.

You called me angry
for loving myself out loud—
no apology, no permit,
no translation allowed.

You called me angry
for grieving what was stolen—
and walking away whole,
my pulse still golden.

But you never saw
the grace it takes
to walk into rooms
where my presence shakes
old walls,
where eyes mismeasure me—
and still, I arrive deliberately.

You didn't count
the silences I swallowed
to keep the peace
you never followed.

You missed the flinches,
the practiced smile,
the bitten tongue
to survive a mile.

You heard my *no*
and named it rage.

But I call it free—
freedom is raising my voice
when told to whisper,
walking from tables
that feed me scraps,
loving myself into a rebuild
the world tried to collapse.

You called me angry—
and maybe I am.
Angry enough not to shrink,
to build a life
you never imagined I'd claim,
to keep rising
while you shovel dirt
on my name.

Call it what you will—
I call it
a flame that outburns the dark,
a drum that drowns the hush,
a woman who won't fold.

I call it free.

## STILL GAY. STILL HERE. STILL UNBOTHERED.

I never saw a rainbow—
not once, not even pressed in glass—
yet I'm gay as fuck.
Never watched two men kiss,
but I dreamed in sapphic hues
long before the word lesbian
was handed to my lips
like a lesson I wasn't meant to pass.

I was raised on Ave Maria
knees raw from pews.
Confession before communion,
mouth stuffed with scripture.
Guilt before breakfast,
heart bruised by a shame
that was never mine
to carry.

I was baptized in your culture—
straight scripts,
Disney spins,
that "when you get a boyfriend" grin.

And yet,
I woke up
every damn day,
queer as ever,
born that way.

So what the fuck
does exposure have to do
with desire—
as if longing

were a billboard
and not a fire?

Where were the gay books,
the teachers,
the cartoons with queer looks?
You can't blame what never showed face
for a truth I carried
like sacred space.

You talk about influence—
as if queerness is a trend,
not a tether, not a lifeline
thrown to a kid trying to bend
in a world that breaks.
As if your discomfort
matters more than a kid
finally finding a mirror
that doesn't distort them.

You're scared of flags.
I'm scared of closets.
One flutters in protest,
the other suffocates in silence.
And only one
has ever left a child
dead—
in their own skin.

I didn't become gay
because I saw a rainbow flag in school.
In fact—
through all of primary and high school,
I never saw one.

Never saw two women kissed.

Never had a gay best friend.
No pride parade,
no queer confession
waiting in the wings.

I've always been this way.
And guess what?
Still gay.
Still here.
Still unbothered.

# THE ONLY ONE IN THE ROOM

I walk in—and suddenly,
the room remembers race.
The silence stiffens,
like it wasn't expecting me
to sit at this table—
let alone speak.

They smile too wide,
ask where I'm from—
like it's small talk—not an audit.
I say, Georgia,
but they want the real answer—
the one seasoned with struggle,
dripping with mangoes and migration,
with stories of boats or borderlines.

I am a checkbox
that checks them—
a diversity goal
with a degree.
They crave my story,
but not my strategy—
my trauma,
not my talent.

Every compliment
feels like a cut:
"You carry yourself so well."
"Not like the others."—
as if I'm a rare breed,
a one-off miracle,
as if we aren't many,
Just exhausted from being unseen.

I make myself small so they can grow.
Water myself down
to survive the meeting.
Speak in tones
that won't echo too loud.
Fold brilliance into bullet points.
Correct them gently
so I'm not the angry one.

And still,
I am studied—
the living syllabus
they didn't sign up for,
learning through me
without permission,
without asking.

But what they forget is:
I'm not just the only one—
I'm the first wave.
The quiet storm.
A presence that teaches without preaching,
challenges without shouting,
makes space
without asking permission.
Because yes,
I am the only one in the room—
but I won't be the last.

# WHERE SILENCE STILL BLEEDS

Silence can be a wound—and our bodies often bear the scar.

These are the poems of a body that disrupts simply by existing. Blackness, queerness, defiance—each one a rebellion against the demand to shrink, to soften, to stay quiet.

Here, every scar is claimed. Every curl, every sway, every survival tactic is named as resistance. These pieces honor the soft and the loud, the quiet that heals and the roar that refuses to fade.

Because sometimes, love is the protest. And sometimes, protest is the most radical form of love we have left.

## LETTER TO THE MIRROR

Not every "yes" is survival—
some are just shape-shifting to fit the frame.
Not every apology keeps you safe;
not every silence is strength—
sometimes, it's surrender in disguise.

The world will teach you early
that vanishing makes you lovable.
They will call it grace—
the way you quiet yourself into corners.
As if folding small enough
could make you easier to hold.
As if disappearing—
could pass for being wanted.

They taught you loud was angry,
silence, a kind of strength.
That softness made you fragile—
and strength was something earned in bruises.
But you were never too loud,
too bold,
too brown—
just uncontainable
in rooms built to blur reflection.
Still, you kept showing up
like a cracked mirror
daring the light to see itself.

You learned to double-knot your boundaries
and call it maturity.
Learned to read the room
faster than your own reflection.
But you deserve rooms

that don't require translation—
where your spirit is already welcome.
And it doesn't need subtitles to belong.

You will tiptoe across tightropes of identity,
where being too much of one thing
meant not enough of another.
You will feel like a visitor
in rooms you were born to belong.
Even those who call you sister
may look at you like a threat—
not because you failed,
but because they were taught
there's only room for one of us to rise.

This is the legacy of divide and rule—
generations taught to confuse proximity to power
with protection.
We were all handed the same rulebook—
the one that said:
divide to survive,
shine alone,
or risk the dark.
So we flinched at each other's rise
instead of rising together.

But you've learned something else:
the soil doesn't compete with the seed—
it holds it,
makes room for it.
Let them call you bitter.
That bitterness was brewed from betrayal,
not born of brokenness.
Your anger and ache—just the taste of memory
when truth has been buried too long.

And even then,
you turned it into poetry—
into purpose,
into presence.
You've outgrown some of our heroes.
You've outlived the limits we once accepted.
You've surprised even yourself
with how deeply you're willing to heal
for the version of you
who still dares to believe in softness.

You've mistaken tight smiles for acceptance.
You've rewritten so many dreams
into smaller, safer versions—
just to be understood.

And I'm proud of us—
not just for surviving,
but for refusing to stop growing
even in cracked soil.

You don't need to be a hero,
a martyr,
or a blueprint for anyone else.
You just need to breathe—
freely,
loudly,
like your breath matters.

You don't need to forgive them to move on.
You don't need to prove we're unbreakable.
You don't have to carry every burden
just because you were strong enough to lift it—
even when the world mistook your silence for shame.

You carry the version of me

who once flinched at her own reflection.
You speak with the voice
I was once too afraid to use.
And with every word,
you stitch yourself back into wholeness.

With love,
the version of us who finally learned
that healing isn't forgetting—
it's remembering without bleeding.
It's facing your own reflection,
standing in your story
without folding.
And today,
I stand for you.

# LETTER TO MY YOUNGER SELF

You don't have to earn your right to rest.
Not with grades, not with silence,
not by being the most helpful in the room.

You don't owe the world your smallness
just to be worthy of love.
You don't have to fold yourself into corners
so others can stand a little taller.

They will tell you to be humble—
but they really mean invisible.
Don't confuse the two.

You'll spend years decoding
which version of you feels safest—
the soft-spoken one, the agreeable one,
the one who laughs while swallowing the sting.

But hear me—
you were never too much.
Your laugh, your dreams, your questions,
your need to cry in the middle of the day—
they were holy.
Still are.

You'll be called angry
before anyone asks you why.
You'll walk into rooms
where your brilliance reads as threat—
even to those who look like you,
even to sisters taught
we can't rise together.

But that's not your burden to fix.

That's the inheritance of a system
designed to divide and conquer
before we even get the chance to bloom.

You were not born to compete
for air or affection.
You were born whole.
Born worthy.
Born vast.

You don't have to dim
so someone else can shine.
You don't need permission
to speak.
To laugh.
To take up space.

Let your softness survive—
let it be your quiet rebellion.
You will learn to rest
without guilt,
to say no
without shame,
to leave
without explaining.

You will one day become the woman
you needed most—
and when you meet her in the mirror,
smiling back at you with no apology,
I hope you finally see:


You've made it.
Not perfect.
But whole.

Still becoming.

Love, Me
From Your Future Self.

# TURN YOUR TONGUE

"Quand on n'a rien à dire,
le mieux est de se taire."
they'd say—
in the soft hush of home,
where silence was sacred,
and words held weight
like wet laundry—heavy,
clung to the chest.

I was told to
turn my tongue
seven times
inside my mouth
before letting it loose—
to measure meaning,
to taste intention,
to pause long enough
to catch regret
before it caught me.

So I learned quiet.
I learned restraint.
I learned that stillness
could be safety,
that thoughtfulness
could be power.

But then I grew up
and sat in rooms
where power dressed loud—
where mouths moved fast
and tongues never turned,
where ignorance echoed
off glass conference walls

and still
got framed as brilliance.

The louder they spoke,
the more they were heard.
Content was optional.
Confidence was king.
I watched wisdom
get confused for whiteness,
and decency mistaken
for diplomacy,
while silence—
my practiced grace—
was mistaken for absence.

Here, it's a world
à l'envers.
Where quiet is weakness
and noise wears the crown.
Where caution is cowardice
and interruption is intellect.

But I still turn my tongue—
not out of fear,
but intention.
Because words are spells.
And I'd rather speak
with the weight of truth
than the volume of ego.

# HEALING DON'T LOOK LIKE SILENCE

They say, "Healing is pensive"—but that lie cuts deeper
than it should.
'Cause peace ain't passive—it's choosing you when no one
else would.

It's choosing you when no one else would.

It doesn't sound like nodding—when you really meant to
scream.
Or quietly shrinking, so someone else gets to dream.

It's choosing you when no one else would.

It's not the quiet girl, trained to never curse,
Or the coiled Black pearl, still clapping in reverse.

It's choosing you when no one else would.

Healing ain't polite—it doesn't stay serene,
It cusses at night—sometimes loud, sometimes obscene.

It's choosing you when no one else would.

It's ugly crying in the car; it's journaling with your fists.
Avoiding Sunday brunch by far, 'cause healing comes with
risks.

It's choosing you when no one else would.

It's telling your mama— 'No, that wasn't okay.'
It's canceling plans to just glow, and breathe your own
way.

It's choosing you when no one else would.

It's therapy and stage: it's screaming through each page so
true.
It's gospel and rage, not bleeding just 'cause they raised
you.

It's choosing you when no one else would.

Healing don't look like silence; it's cutting the cord with no
reply.
It's dodging his daily ignorance and not explaining why.

It's choosing you when no one else would.

It looks like side-eyes at work, but I still walk high.
With poise and petty smirk, I laugh, not lie.

It's choosing you when no one else would.

To dance barefoot—through ancestral rain, unafraid.
To unlearn shame's root, that your body never made.

It's choosing you when no one else would.

It's honoring the fire, even where your skin's been turned.
To walk through the pyre, with scars you've earned.

It's choosing you when no one else would.

So don't tell me to be quiet—now that I've found my voice.
I won't shrink to fit your diet, this rage is my choice.

It's choosing you when no one else would.

This softness? This thunder?—not a phase, not a ploy.

It's sacred, it's coming from deep under; it's survival, not joy.

It's choosing you when no one else would.

N.A. Homie's healing? —don't mistake it for silence.
It echoes without needing—permissionless resilience.

It's choosing you when no one else would.

# GUILTY BY SILENCE

Will I be on the first plane to voidness, for shattering
stillness?
For refusing to wear silence like a funeral dress, for
shattering stillness?

Will I be exiled on the first boat to wilderness
for daring to demand human sacredness, for shattering
stillness?

Will I make the next headline for exposing your harshness
then silenced in exile's darkness, for shattering stillness?

Will you label me guilty for naming your tone-deafness,
while you bask in migrants' distress, sealed in caged
coldness, for shattering stillness?

On the far side of fear's imposed weakness,
how complicit am I if I bow to this madness, for shattering
stillness?

How complicit am I to carry witness to your weakness,
yet hush the truth, fearing your crafted bleakness, for
shattering stillness?

Staying quiet while your cruelty feeds the vulnerable's
madness,
letting guilt rot me slow, turning silence to illness, for
shattering stillness.

How much blood will stain my hands without forgiveness,
if I stay silent, feeding despair's darkness, for shattering
stillness?

Fear is the cunning tool to forge collective deafness,

as guilty silence drags my soul toward helplessness, for
shattering stillness.

If fear stitches silence as strengthless neatness,
am I complicit for sparing the madness, for shattering
stillness?

I won't be paralyzed while my kin vanish in caged
bleakness,
even if I'm brutalized in solitary boldness, for shattering
stillness.

N.A. Homie will pin verses to disturb the guilty stillness;
I refuse to be guilty by silence's madness, for shattering
stillness.

# YOU NEVER READ, YOU JUST REPEAT

For all your loud, unfounded claims,
you never cite real facts or names.
Not the meme. Not the preacher.
Not your cousin's podcast screecher.

Where's your source? Where's the research?
Where's the data you didn't just search?
Not your cousin's TikTok-fueled eruption—
just recycled fear and weak assumption.

Where's the pause before you parrot fear with no aim?
"Gay men are made in prison," you proudly claim.
"Lesbians were assaulted"—you echo that shame.
"Rainbows confuse kids"—your favorite blame.

I've studied trauma, identity, the science you ignore—
peer-reviewed pages you'd never explore.
But you watched YouTube clips, all the facts blurred,
then claimed expertise you never earned.

I've sat with scholars, sifted through thick debates,
traced history's roots, untangled coded hate.
I've mapped what fear distorts, and truth reveals—
not every story fits your highlight reels.

You skim headlines and call it a case closed,
chase echo chambers where bias is exposed.
Then shout your half-truths like they've been earned—
still quoting sources you've never even learned.

You never stop to ask whose voice you've made your own,
or question if that echo was ever yours alone.
You speak with such conviction, but truth gets excluded—
I've studied every angle—even yours—concluded.

I've weighed both sides, yours, too, I've dissected,
challenged my bias, not just what's expected.
But you've never read a voice outside your sphere.
just those who preach the things you already fear.

You think loud means right—volume = validity.
But shouting your bias just exposes your fragility.
So next time you speak with your facts misread,
try opening a book before opening your head.

# FIVE SECONDS OF EMPATHY

You gave me five seconds.
Five borrowed seconds
of borrowed grief
on borrowed time.

You posted the headline,
captioned it with a broken heart
like that emoji could hold the weight
of a mother's scream.

You said,
"This is so heartbreaking."
"This is not who we are."
"This can't keep happening."
But then—
it kept happening.
And you didn't.

You hit share,
then hit brunch.
Said "We need change,"
then changed the subject.
Said "I stand with…"
but only long enough
for the likes to peak.

Your activism had a timer.
And mine?
Mine has receipts.
Of who showed up.
Who stayed loud
after the timeline moved on.
After our hashtags stopped trending
but our grief didn't.

You borrowed my pain
like a book you never finished.
Used my story
as a backdrop
for your moral glow-up.
Then dropped it
once the heat died down.

You reposted George.
Muted Breonna.
Ignored Sudan.
Skipped Haiti.
Said Gaza was "too political."
Said voting "felt like a lot."
Said justice was your vibe
until the merch got too messy.

You said "Black Lives Matter"—
but not at work,
not in your HOA,
not when your uncle cracked that joke
and you just laughed.

Five seconds.
That's all I get
before the curtain closes,
the feed refreshes,
and you're back to oat milk and outfit checks.

But I'm still here.
Off-screen.
Off-trend.
Out of your borrowed time.
And still—
still fighting to be more
than your fleeting empathy.

# WALK A DAY IN MY SHOES

Walk a day in my shoes—not the ones you paint as right,
but the ones caked in dirt from dawn's first scroll.
They've fled from hands that clawed in the night,
so worn, every stone cuts straight through my soul.

 But the ones caked in dirt from dawn's first scroll.
Worn not by choice, but stitched for survival.
These shoes climbed trees, each crate a crushing toll—
though pain cracked bone by bone, I denied the spiral.

Worn not by choice, but stitched for survival.
Better pain than to be some predator's tool—
better bones shattered in fields of denial
than to rot in a system that names itself the rule.

Better pain than to be some predator's tool—
So, I ran from gunfire, from fear's cruel contrarian.
You let me in—not out of care, but to play a role,
a border pass you waved, to crown yourself humanitarian.

So, I ran from gunfire, from fear's cruel contrarian.
Then I got here. I conformed. I smiled too much.
I softened my accent, waited like a good egalitarian—
grateful my body was no longer a target or a crutch.

Then I got here. I conformed. I smiled too much.
Despite my compliance, you still marked me criminal.
I swallowed my pride, my accent—my clutch—
just hoping you'd repaint the lens of my arrival.

Despite my compliance, you still marked me criminal.
 You stand by false values but erase my dignity.
Once, I was a doctor—respected, not minimal—
now I scrub your floors to soothe my home's misery.

You stand by false values but erase my dignity.
Though I'm grateful, don't mistake that for blindness to
your unfairness.
My degrees meant something—until I became your
property,
while you praise my mop but dismiss my distress.

Though I'm grateful, don't mistake that for blindness to
your unfairness.
I dare you to walk a day in my shoes and still think I'm less
than.
Try standing tall while your dreams rot in blissful
unawareness,
 smiling through grief while they pretend your pain was
part of the plan.

 I dare you to walk a day in my shoes and still think I'm
less than.
To walk through a day where all you know is unknown.
Still, I show up to clean, to serve, to smile again—
you wouldn't last a few hours before it's all blown.

To walk through a day where all you know is unknown.
But I can't afford to fall—I carry someone else's gleam
Walk a day in my shoes and find out on your own:
am I less—or are you just a moron too blind to see my
dream?

Walk a day in my shoes—not the ones you paint as right,
But I can't afford to fall—I carry someone else's gleam.
They've fled from hands that clawed in the night,
 Am I less—or are you just too blind to see my dream?

# THE SKY WE MAKE

The storm has passed, but the air still hums with electricity.

These are the poems of what comes after—when the fight for survival becomes the work of creation. When we lift our eyes, see what's above us, and decide to shape it together.

This is joy that remembers where it came from. Hope that doesn't pretend the wound is gone. This is grief holding hands with possibility.

This is the sky we make together.

# STILL HERE. STILL HUMAN.

I walked in limping—chest tight, skin pale,
But you checked my ID before hearing my tale.
A name you stumbled through at first sight
Was enough to erase my human light.

I spoke in English, wore my smile thin,
But you saw foreignness beneath my skin.
"Insurance?" you asked—never my name—
As if my right to live was part of a game.

The nurse tapped quick on a flickering screen,
Reduced to data—barely seen.
You chart my pain with practiced flair,
Yet never ask what brought me there.

I was taught to sit straight, to not take up space,
To whisper "thank you" while bleeding, just to save face.
But quiet isn't safe—I've learned firsthand,
Silence can kill more than what's scanned.

I've survived war zones without sounds,
Now I endure microaggressions that cut like rounds.
My blood type unchanged since crossing your gate,
Yet you still treat my pain as second-rate.

Still here. Still breathing. Still won't bend—
Even as stories like mine are forced to an end.
Even when protests fade from the screen,
And prayers replace aid and hope to demean.

Still human—though you skim past my chart,
Though you check my vitals, not my heart.
Still dreaming, even as you conspire
To tuck our stories in funeral choirs.

# WHERE I CARRY MY JOY

Hate tried to bury my laughter beneath survival,
But still, I rise—I carry my joy with ancestral pride.

I carry my joy with ancestral pride.

I carry my joy in a chipped coffee mug,
the one that's seen every Monday shrug.

I carry my joy with ancestral pride.

In rice and beans that fill my plate,
in mango slices sweet and late.

I carry my joy with ancestral pride.

Tucked in Sunday hair, freshly braided,
by hands that heal what the world degraded.

I carry my joy with ancestral pride.

In dollar-store gloss and thrifted gold,
in stories my grandma always told.

I carry my joy with ancestral pride.

In porchlight dances, no witness near,
just laughter loud enough to hear.

I carry my joy with ancestral pride.

In creased-up notes and playlists loud,
in singing off-key, still feeling proud.

I carry my joy with ancestral pride.

It lives in texts from friends who check,
in candles lit without a prayer to direct—

I carry my joy with ancestral pride.

Joy's not what I buy or prove—
it's the silence I choose not to move.

I carry my joy with ancestral pride.

It's knowing I'm magic, messy, whole—
a walking poem with a fire-scarred soul.

I carry my joy with ancestral pride.

I carry my joy where grief can't steal,
beneath the wounds that never heal.

I carry my joy with ancestral pride.

In hips that sway through every no,
in choosing softness just to grow.

I carry my joy with ancestral pride.

So if you ask me where joy stays—
it's in my feet, my lips, my gaze.

I carry my joy with ancestral pride.

N.A. Homie is not just surviving, but painting skies,
in colors no empire can sanitize.

I carry my joy with ancestral pride.

## WERE THE HASHTAG, THEN THE FOOTNOTE

You wore the blue bracelet
after Election Day—
a bead of borrowed allyship,
to say "I'm not part of that 53%"—
but made no call,
sent no check,
spoke no truth,
to the hands that cast our undoing.

We were the headline,
the rally cry,
the blacked-out square
you swore redeemed you.
You typed our names
with trembling thumbs—
whispered them twice
like a spell
to shield yourself
from shame

You made us a moment,
then you made us quiet.
Folded our pain
into cropped and curated memories.
Archived the outrage,
buried the receipts,
and scrolled on
to the next crisis
with cleaner filters.

We watched you weep
on stories that expired.
Watched your timeline

turn tranquil—
while we stayed in the trenches,
still fighting,
still naming the dead,
still waking to sirens
and injustice in our skies.

You said,
"Don't forget their names."
But yours was the voice
that fell quiet first.
Your silence
echoed louder than protest—
your comfort
always found
the nearest exit.

Now when we speak,
you flinch—like we're loud again.
Like we've overstayed
our viral welcome.
But our stories don't expire.
Our grief doesn't fade
just because you did.


We were the hashtag.
Now we're a hyperlink—
tucked at the bottom of your syllabus.
A bullet point
in your company's Diversity Month memo.
A memory
you'd rather keep closed.

But we
were never a trend.

We were the truth
you couldn't carry.
And we are still here—
louder,
longer,
unerasable.

We are not hashtags
for you to flatten
into footnotes.

# THE FLAG YOU FEAR MIGHT SAVE A LIFE

Do you know,
maybe
that rainbow flag,
hanging quiet
in the hallway,
might be the one thing
that saves
a child's
life?

That maybe—
just maybe—
some little queer kid
sees it
and finally knows
they're not
the only one.
That they don't have to die
in silence,
don't have to
bury themselves
just to make
you
comfortable.

Funny,
how your motto toggles between:
"I can accept you,
but I don't have to respect you,"
or is it—
"I can respect you,
but I don't have to accept you
who you are"?

Either way,
it's still rejection
dressed in
decorum.

Who the hell are you
to treat acceptance like a favor?
You think respect and acceptance
can walk different roads—
but they can't.
Not when we're talking
basic.
human.
dignity.

And I got loud.
Got fire-throated.
Defending queer kids
clinging to rainbows like life vests
in seas that want to drown them.
Defending caged men
whose bodies were broken,
then branded—
as if assault could rewrite desire.
Defending women like me,
tired of being told
our queerness is smoke
from someone else's fire—
not the spark
we were born with.

I'm not just gay.
I'm layered—
a symphony of selves,
brilliant in ways you've never bothered to name.
But somehow,

that one note in my song
is the only one you hear
when it's time to cast blame,
to ink injustice into law,
to hang your hatred like scripture
from the rafters of a pulpit.

Where do you get your truth from?
Because I feast on journals—
peer-reviewed, sharp as scalpels,
cutting through myth with method.
And you?
You sip from fear-fed headlines,
scrolling for validation
in echo chambers
where bias is baptized
and facts are optional.

You only read what kisses your bias—
what tucks your fear in at night
and calls it fact.
That's not learning—
that's indoctrination
in a comfort-colored cloak.

You claim kids raised by gay parents
will turn out gay.
Like queerness rubs off
like glitter from a pride parade.
But study after study
peels that lie clean—
not once,
not twice,
but every damn time
truth stood trial.

Still—
if truth can't touch you,
what am I even doing?

Then I remembered:
You cast your ballot
for silence,
for ongoing oppression.
I cast mine
for breath,
for peace—
for a glimpse of light
through the crack.

# YOUR RAINBOW WAS SEASONAL

Your pride was a profile pic,
then poof—forgotten quick.
That rainbow you posted?
It faded with the trending topic.
You wore it like a summer shirt,
then folded it up
once the headlines stopped hurting.

You said "Love is love"
until your church said "Not here."
You clapped at the wedding
but flinched at the kiss.
You shared our joy
but muted our grief.
You loved our "Yas queen!"
but not our "Please help."

Your rainbow was seasonal—
June's default filter.
Then July came,
and you're back to neutral.

You used our pain to sell tees,
built brands off our bravery,
then asked us to keep it tasteful
when the office lunch got too quiet.

You watched our rights
get peeled back like tape,
and whispered,
"Well... it's complicated."

You mean—
it's complicated to care

when the merch is gone,
the vibe is off,
and we're not so palatable
without glitter?

You meant to say,
"I loved you best
when you weren't asking for anything."
But we were.
We still are.

Because we're still here.
Still married. Still fired.
Still raising kids. Still buried.
Still targeted. Still brilliant.
Still not "too much" to deserve safety.

So don't call it allyship
if your love had an expiration.
Don't say you marched
if you walked away
as soon as the flag
clashed with your feed.

We don't need your rainbow
if it's only weather-based.
We need your spine.
Your vote.
Your voice.
Your seat flipped at the dinner table
when someone says we don't belong.

Your rainbow is seasonal.
Ours is survival.
Year-round.
Storm-tested.

Still flying.

# WHEN THE CAUSE BECOMES UNCOOL

You marched when it matched your feed.
Held signs like props,
posed just right—
#JusticeInLighting.
Black and white,
but mostly white
beneath the ring light.

You wore the shirt,
until it clashed
with your brunch plans.
Posted the quote,
until it slowed
your engagement stats.
Gave a damn,
until damn wasn't cute anymore.

We were the statement piece
for your season of "woke."
Aesthetic empathy.
Limited edition concern.
Now we're clearance rack casualties,
unfollowed and folded
behind your new pastel cause.

Remember when rage
was trending?
When you wept performatively
in curated reels?
When you practiced pronouns
like lines in a play
you never meant to finish?

Our lives aren't a phase.

Not a pop-up shop
for your moral glow-up.
We still carry grief
like second skin—
you carry guilt
like last year's accessory.

So don't come back
when the hashtags rotate.
Don't repost us
when the next Black death
goes viral.
We were always bleeding—
you just stopped watching.

# YOUR ALLYSHIP EXPIRED LAST WEEK

You wore the shirt, posted the square,
Learned the lingo — just enough to care.
You hashtagged justice, marched one mile,
Then ghosted truth with a curated smile.

Your timeline held my grief in June,
Then left it out to dry too soon.
Solidarity's not a seasonal flair—
It's not a coat you wear when it's in the air.

You practiced pronouns like a prayer,
Until it clashed with your daddy's glare.
You loved us loud when it cost you none,
But silence came once the heat begun.

Your allyship expired the moment it got hard—
When truth turned sharp and comfort felt scarred.
When silence seemed safer than standing near,
You clocked out the second it cost you fear.

Ally's not a badge you keep on file,
It's risk. It's blistered feet while walking that mile.
It's showing up when no one sees,
It's holding space, not just retweets.

You loved us when we were tragic, bold —
Not when we're angry, weary, or old.
Your comfort always outweighed the truth,
Your allyship? A half-used booth.

So miss me with that "I still care" line—
You dipped the moment it cost a spine.
You don't get to brand my fight as chic—
Your allyship expired last week.

# MADE IN AMERICA, UNDONE AT THE BORDER

I was made in America, but undone at the border.
My first breath was pledged to the land of the free.
I called her mother—this country, my order—
I knew this land before I knew me.

I learned Buenos Días—my parents never mastered
Spanglish.
Their words flew fast for my small tongue to keep pace.
But I understood enough to know I wasn't foolish
To call this land my home, to proudly claim my place.

I grew up speaking your language and my parents'
language.
I turned my own into a mash of both—a survival code.
When I say "that's sick," my parents just can't manage
When I say "oye," you think it's short for Ovaltine mode.

My language stitched from struggle, sass, and spite.
A hybrid tongue too bold to break, too fierce to drag.
I pledged allegiance every morning with fearless might,
Until I learned this home won't let me plant my flag.

I didn't know I didn't belong—until you said I wasn't
American.
Not until the flashing lights, the questions sharp and thin.
Not until the cuffs rewrote my story with no plan
America was mine—until it shut me out again, with a cruel
grin.

Dreamer. That's the label they stamped when I stalled.
DACA—a hollow acronym my lawyer tried to explain.
Now I spiral in silence, by fear enthralled.

This home was never mine—my truth dismissed again, like a stain.

So tell me—do I belong on the other side of the border,
Where I don't speak the tongue or know their layered culture?
I can't move like them, can't mirror their order,
They call me foreign too—just an outsider, not fit in their structure.

What did I do wrong—besides being born past the wrong borderline?
I put my head down, did everything right to make everyone proud.
I got degrees, I got the grind, kept walking your straight line,
But still, I'm shut out—too foreign for your crowd.

If I don't belong here—where I took my first step, whispered my first hi,
Why am I aching for a home they said wasn't mine all along?
Why won't someone slow down, look back, and tell me why?
Can someone help me solve it—just tell me where I belong?

# Acknowledgments

This book was not written in isolation. It was carried here by the hands, hearts, and histories of many.

To my family—thank you for holding space for my voice, even when it trembled, even when the truths I carried were heavy. You taught me that survival is a form of poetry, and that love is a kind of rebellion.

To the friends who listened to early drafts, who reminded me that my words mattered when doubt was loud—you kept me tethered to the page. Your faith was a quiet light in the long nights.

To the communities I belong to—immigrant, Black, queer—this is for you. You have shown me resilience that no system can erase. I hope these poems reflect even a fraction of your beauty, your fight, and your brilliance.

To the elders, teachers, and poets who came before me—you built the road I now walk. Your courage made space for mine.

And to every reader who finds themselves in these pages: thank you for letting my voice meet yours. May these poems meet you where you are, and remind you that you are never alone in the telling.

And to the ancestors—named and unnamed—whose strength moves through my bones: this is your echo, carried forward.

# Author's Note

I didn't write this book to be polite.
I wrote it because I was tired—of headlines that
numbed, of hashtags that faded, of silence being
mistaken for peace. These poems are stitched from
protest and tenderness, rage and reclamation. They are
the stories I couldn't swallow anymore, the truths I
needed to speak out loud.

This collection holds more than language—it holds
memory, identity, resistance. It honors the ways we
survive and the ways we dream beyond survival. It's a
love letter to those who've been told they're too much,
too loud, too foreign, too queer, too dark, too difficult
to love.

In these pages, you'll find pain, yes—but also joy,
laughter, softness, and fire. Because we are not just
what has happened to us. We are what we choose to
make of it.

Thank you for reading. For witnessing. For carrying
some of this with me.

In power and in poetry,
N.A. Homie

# The Ember-Ghazal Guide

The ember-ghazal was born from fire—its flicker, its survival, its truth. It is my reclamation of the traditional Persian ghazal, shaped by the breath of diaspora, protest, and inherited resilience.

Where classical ghazals echo with longing, mine burn with memory. I kept the spine of the form: the repeated refrain, the couplet structure, the rhythm of return. But I stripped away what didn't serve my voice—rigid meter, imposed rhyme—and replaced it with my own: a language that limps, laughs, testifies.

Each ember-ghazal carries a line like a scar or a mantra, returning again and again—not for beauty, but for insistence. For the need to say it one more time. To be believed. To refuse erasure.

**Traditional Ghazal Structure (in brief):**
Written in couplets (two-line stanzas)
Each couplet is autonomous (can stand alone)
The second line of every couplet ends with the same **refrain**
The word before the refrain **rhymes**
Often includes the poet's name or signature in the final stanza

**The Ember-Ghazal Modification:**
Refrain is retained, but rhyme is optional
Repetition is spiritual, emotional—not decorative
Poem builds cumulative emotional weight, not disjointed fragments
Final stanza often shifts from communal voice to personal or prophetic

**Example (from *Where I Carry My Joy*):**
I carry my joy in a chipped coffee mug,

the one that's seen every Monday shrug.
*I carry my joy with ancestral pride.*
In rice and beans that fill my plate,
in mango slices sweet and late.
*I carry my joy with ancestral pride.*
The repetition is not just stylistic—it insists. It carries
history. It becomes liturgy.
These poems repeat because we've been ignored. They
return because history does. They hold the tension
between what we survive and what we're still owed.
May they be read like chants, like testimony, like
breath refusing to be held.
—*N.A. Homie*

## About the Author

N.A. Homie is a poet, therapist, and community advocate whose work weaves lived experience with unflinching truth. Her writing moves between protest and prayer, blending the personal with the political to reveal the resilience and beauty of marginalized voices.

Drawing from her Haitian roots, her work in mental health, and her years of grassroots organizing, she writes with a deep understanding of survival, identity, and joy as forms of resistance. Her poems have been shared in community spaces, healing circles, and cultural events, resonating with readers who see their own truths reflected in her words.

*Illegals* is her debut collection, a testament to the belief that stories—when spoken boldly—can change how we see each other and ourselves.

*Swim Lessons* is Maud Lavin's radiant meditation on being alive, and the radical freedom of choosing one's own strokes. Part conservation, part love letter, and part memoir, this book flows through Chicago's 57th Street Beach and beyond, tracing the kinetic beat of swimmers delighting in becoming mermaids in the sand, tarot card magic, sex in a New York park, and a humid Singapore evening with the promise of water. In the waves of memory and motion, Lavin crafts a love letter to a life lived expansively on land and in water, embracing the power of self-reclamation at any age.

—**Dipika Mukherjee, author of** *Dialect of Distant Harbors,* *Writer's Postcards,* **and other works**

In *Swim Lessons*, Maud Lavin writes "The Midwest was my first love," and this collection shows us what it looks like when a first love matures. What I particularly love about this book is how Lavin champions boredom—in this listless state, or where small loves have room to grow into endless, shimmering horizons. Lavin invites us on a journey through the Midwest, and in each city, the speaker's admiration for water ripples through. Each lake that we encounter is a basin of memory, a mirror in which previous versions of the speaker float to the surface before disappearing again. Most importantly, the lakes serve as models of hunger and desire, of how to hold the people we love, of how to swallow what we want whole.

—**Taylor Byas, author of** *Resting Bitch Face*

Maud Lavin's *Swim Lessons* is an ebullient, loving, plainspoken song about pleasure. Here, swimming, sex, and flying are central modes of inquiry about topics ranging from aging to bigotry, the Midwest's lush greenery and it's "small-town small heart," to the body and its connection to nature. In "Forever Water," Lavin posits a fantasy of a lake that "feels clean," despite forever chemicals; in "Spell" the reader is carried by the inimitable rhythm of swimming "my left knee rocks, meniscus/..." In gorgeous watery moments we read a voice in love with experience, "to know life is friable and devote mine to love,/" she writes in this joyful poetry debut.

—**Thea Goodman, author of** *The Invented Mother*